D0231471

THE HOLY SPIRIT, OUR COUNSELLOR

SELWYN HUGHES

THE HOLY SPIRIT, OUR COUNSELLOR

CWR

Originally published as *Every Day with Jesus, The Divine Counsellor*
May/June 1995 by CWR. This new revised edition published 2004 by
CWR, Waverley Abbey House, Waverley Lane, Farnham, Surrey GU9
8EP.

See back of book for list of National Distributors.

Unless otherwise indicated, all Scripture references are from the
Holy Bible: New International Version (NIV), copyright © 1973,
1978, 1984 by the International Bible Society.
Other versions used:
Moffatt: *The Moffatt Translation of the Bible*, © 1987, Hodder &
Stoughton

Front cover image: Image Bank

Concept development, editing, design and production by CWR

Printed in Spain by Zure

ISBN: 1-85345-309-9

CONTENTS

INTRODUCTION

We will be focusing in this book on Christ's famous utterance in which He describes the Holy Spirit as the divine Counsellor (John 14:16). But first let me set the scene.

It is the night before Christ is to be crucified, and He is closeted with His disciples in an upper room in the sacred city of Jerusalem. The air is heavy with the atmosphere of imminent events. The Passover has been celebrated, Judas has just left, and suddenly Christ announces that He is soon to leave this world and return to His Father in heaven. We read these words of our Lord with calmness, but I can imagine that when they were first spoken the disciples were anything but calm. Their stomachs must have churned within them as they heard their Master say He was going away. For over three years He had been their Teacher, their Confidante and their Guide. He had comforted them when they were sad, inspired them in times of doubt, and encouraged them whenever their footsteps began to flag. He had been to them a Counsellor par excellence. But now He was going. How were they to handle things in His absence? What were they to do when they didn't know which course of action to take? Who was to be their inspiration and guide? Another Counsellor is to take His place, He informs them – the blessed Holy Spirit.

The Spirit came, as we know, at Pentecost, to be to the

disciples all that Jesus was – and more. And He has remained in the world to be our Counsellor too. But how dependent are we on His counsel? How often do we draw on His resources? Sadly, all too seldom and too little. God has appointed a divine Counsellor to assist us, yet so often we prefer to muddle along on our own.

CHAPTER ONE

A DIVINE COUNSELLOR

John 1:29–34; 14:1–17, 18–31
Acts 16:1–10
James 1:1–11

'And I will ask the Father, and he will give you another
Counsellor to be with you for ever – the Spirit of truth'
John 14:16

The statement 'I will ask the Father, and he will give you another Counsellor' is found in the section of John's Gospel known as 'The Upper Room Discourse' – chapters 14 to 16. Think with me again about how the news that Christ was leaving the world to go to the Father would have been received by the disciples. For more than three years they had been inseparable. When they went to sleep at night they knew that He would be there in the morning to lead and inspire them. Now all that was about to change – for ever. No more meals together, no more quiet talks around the camp fire at night, no more shared laughter, no more deep spiritual discussions.

Speaking of His departure from the world, our Lord used the word 'orphans' (John 14:18). Why orphans? The disciples were adults, not children. Ah, the sting of His departure left them feeling as bereft as a child who has lost both parents. Yet His promise, remember, was not to leave them as orphans. I am sure it was difficult for the disciples to believe at that time that they would ever get over the feelings they experienced as they heard their Master was going away, but subsequent events show that they did overcome them.

When the Holy Spirit visited them at Pentecost the

Jesus had been with them, but the Holy Spirit was in them and would remain in them.

dispirited disciples came alive again, and appeared to become twice the men they were when Jesus was with them. Why? The answer is quite simple. Jesus had been *with* them, but the Holy Spirit was *in* them and would remain in them. There was no fear that *He* might go away. He would remain with them always. And what He was to them He is to us also – *a permanent presence.*

With you forever

When Jesus announced that the divine Counsellor would abide with His disciples permanently (and subsequently with the whole Church), keep in mind that

The Holy Spirit is a Counsellor who is available every day and all day.

it had never been like this before, not even in the lives of the Old Testament greats. But from now on ... yes! Remember too that the pattern the disciples had of the coming of the Holy Spirit, as seen in the Old Testament, was of temporary endowments of power for temporary tasks. In other words, He came and went. Yet in John 14:16–17, Jesus announced that following His return to the throne in heaven the Holy Spirit's coming would be permanent.

This foreverness of the Spirit is intimated in John 1:33. Note the words 'and remain'. These words and the phrase used in John 14:16 – 'to be with you for ever' – strike the same note. The idea of an occasional visitation is replaced by a permanent coming.

The Holy Spirit is a Counsellor who is available every day and all day. Human counsellors have to set aside special times to see people and often have difficulty in fitting everyone into their schedules. This, however, is not a problem to the divine Counsellor. You can approach Him any time of night or day, and though He may be involved at the same time in counselling thousands of your fellow believers, He will give Himself to you as if you were the only one on the face of the planet. And you don't have to look for Him in any other place than in your own heart. The Holy Spirit is not only the divine Counsellor but a dependable Counsellor. He is available to you and me – permanently.

Another Counsellor

Permit me to remind you again of our Lord's words: 'I will ask the Father, and he will give you another Counsellor' (John 14:16). Note the word *another*. Without that word we have no point of comparison; the word 'Counsellor' would be unanchored. Counsels us how? And to do what? He counsels us in the same way and with the same principles that Christ followed when He counselled His disciples. The Spirit's counsel was to be the same as Jesus' counsel. In the very nature of things it could not be different.

In Acts 16:6–7, notice that the terms 'Holy Spirit' and 'Spirit of Jesus' are used interchangeably? Look at it again: 'having been kept by the Holy Spirit from preaching the word' (v.6), and 'the Spirit of Jesus would not allow them to' (v.7). The Holy Spirit seemed to the disciples to be the Spirit of Jesus within them. They were one. The counsel given to every believer by the Holy Spirit will accord with the counsel given to the disciples by Jesus when He was here on earth. If God is a Christlike God, then the Spirit is a Christlike Spirit.

There are many matters about which I know little or nothing, but one thing I do know about is counselling as I have been involved in it for over 40 years. When I meet a counsellor I can usually tell what school of thought he or she belongs to by listening to that person talk. It is the same with the Holy Spirit. Having observed how He functions in the lives of men and women (and in my own life) over the years, I can tell what school He comes from. It is the 'The Jesus School of Counselling'. He counsels in the same way as Christ.

The first thing
Our heavenly Father has given us the Holy Spirit to be our Counsellor yet how much do we avail ourselves of His resources? All across the world the Christian Church is going through what has been called a 'counselling explosion'. While this has many benefits, the danger is that we put our faith in human counsellors rather than in the divine Counsellor.

I remember a time in the Church when counselling was

regarded by many as an unnecessary ministry. If you have a problem, it was said at that time, never look to others for help; instead, get down on your knees and talk to God about it – the Holy Spirit will show you what to do. That, of course, was an extreme position. Often it does help to talk through a problem with a Christian counsellor. As David Seamands puts it: 'a counsellor [ie, a Christian counsellor] is a temporary assistant to the Holy Spirit.' But the Church nowadays seems to be going to the opposite extreme by suggesting that when anyone has a problem the first thing they should do is to discuss it with a Christian counsellor.

> The first thing we should do ... is turn to the divine Counsellor and invite Him to help.

No, the first thing we should do whenever we have a problem that cannot be solved using our own resources is to turn to the divine Counsellor and invite Him to help us (see James 1:5). If light does not come then seek the help of a wise and godly friend. But seeking help from others should not be our first recourse; our first recourse should be to God. The Holy Spirit, as we said, is a Counsellor par excellence. To seek counselling from another Christian is, of course, quite valid, but that kind of counselling might be needed less if we depended on the Holy Spirit more.

We are in danger of falling into the trap of taking our

problems first to a Christian counsellor rather than bringing them straight to God. Why do we do this?

There are many possible reasons. Maybe we prefer a visible counsellor to an invisible one. Perhaps we are not sure how to establish contact with the divine Counsellor or how to recognise His voice when He speaks to us. Or possibly we are not quite certain that the divine Counsellor is interested in the likes of us. We can believe He guides and counsels such people as Billy Graham, Luis Palau or Mother Teresa – but ordinary people like us? Ah, that's different.

It is these issues and many others that I want to come to grips with, but let me lay this down in your mind right away: the services of the divine Counsellor are yours for the asking. If you are a Christian then His resources are available to you – free and for the taking. It is customary for anyone who is charged with an offence and brought to court to have a professional advocate to counsel them and plead their case. If they cannot afford one, one is provided for them – free of charge. God and Christ do for you, as one of His children, what any good government will do; they provide you with counsel. When we spurn the services of the divine Counsellor we grieve Him (see Eph. 4:30). For He is not merely an influence; He is a *Person*.

> For He is not merely an influence; He is a *Person*.

'He' – not 'It'

This is why, when we talk about Him, we must refer to Him as 'He' and not 'it'. Some Christians believe He is an impersonal influence yet use personal pronouns such as 'He' and 'His' when referring to Him. I remember on one occasion pointing out the illogicality of this to someone who held this view, and this was his reply: 'I use a personal pronoun when talking about the Holy Spirit in the same way that people use the term "Jack Frost" when speaking about icy conditions.' What nonsense.

The Holy Spirit is not the personification of an influence, the sense of fellowship Christians experience when they get together, or even spiritual enthusiasm. He is a Person in the same way that you and I are persons – only of course much more so. He has individuality, intelligence, hearing, knowledge, wisdom, sympathy, and so on. He can see, speak, rejoice, love, whisper, and, as we have seen, when we spurn Him by turning to other resources, or resist Him when He seeks to work within us, He is grieved in the same way that a close friend would be hurt. The Bible says He is God, with the very same attributes as God. In Job 26:13 He is seen as having the power to create. In Psalm 139:7 He is shown to have omnipresence – being everywhere present. In Hebrews 3:7 He is spoken of as issuing commands – something only God can do. And in 2 Corinthians 3:17 He is referred to as 'Lord'.

My dear friend, if you are a Christian there is an unseen deity in your life – the Holy Spirit. He doesn't want to hide from you, and He doesn't want you to hide from Him.

Further Study

1 Kings 22:5; Psa. 16:7; Prov. 3:5–6; Isa. 55:8–9
1. How should we approach God for counsel?
2. Why do we need God as Counsellor?

Isa. 11:1–5; Luke 4:14–19; Rom. 8:9
3. How does the Spirit equip the Messiah?
4. How do we know we belong to Christ?

Psa. 1:1–3; 1 John 1:9; 2:1–2; Rom. 8:5–6
5. Where did the psalmist get counsel?
6. How does God deal with our sin?

CHAPTER TWO

AS CHRIST SEES US

Genesis 17:1–16; 35:1–15
John 1:35–42
2 Corinthians 3:17–18

*'And we, who with unveiled faces all reflect
the Lord's glory, are being transformed into his
likeness with ever-increasing glory, which comes
from the Lord, who is the Spirit.'*
2 Corinthians 3:18

Before we move on to compare the Holy Spirit's counselling ministry with Christ's – particularly as it relates to helping us become the kind of person God sees that we can be – we must ask ourselves the question: To whom do we refer when we describe ourselves by the personal pronoun 'I'? In our personalities is there anything so constant and reliable that we can honestly refer to it as 'I'?

'Human nature is so changeful,' said one philosopher, 'and so subject to swiftly alternating moods, that when I say "I", I am not sure what "I" I am talking about.' Who is the real man or real woman? The man who sings heartily in church and then shouts at his wife and family on the way home in the car? The woman who teaches a Sunday school class and is sweetness and light, or the woman who blows her top when the meal she has prepared for her family turns out all wrong? The same person can be so many different persons. Whom do others mean when they say 'you', and whom do you mean when you say 'I'?

The same person can be so many different persons.

Aristotle claimed there were six different Aristotles. Faust declared: 'Two souls, alas, dwell in this breast of mine.' Renan, the French author, admitted: 'I am two people; one part of me laughs while the other part of me cries.' Even Paul talks about another self dwelling within him (Rom. 7:7–25).

Some might explain this as schizophrenia or 'dual personality', but the elements of what we are talking about are in us all. The real 'you', so I believe, is not the person others see, not even the person you see, but the person God, Christ and the Holy Spirit see. Only they know the real you.

Double vision

If, as we have said, the Holy Spirit is our Counsellor, then what are some of the ways in which He makes His counsel available to us? How does He go about this important task? We pointed out earlier that when Jesus said, 'The Father ... will give you *another* Counsellor,' He meant that the Holy Spirit would counsel us in the same way that Jesus counselled His disciples. So if we can see something of the way Jesus counselled them, we will have a clearer picture of how the Holy Spirit goes about the task of counselling us.

Take first the way in which our Lord came alongside Simon Peter, described in John 1:35–42, and sought to help him see himself as the man he could be. One of the characteristics of a good counsellor is to have a clear vision of a person's potential so that they can encourage that person to move towards it. By potential I mean not so much human potential but our potential in Christ. Jesus looked at Simon and declared: '"You are Simon ... You will be called Cephas" (which, when translated, is Peter).' What was Jesus really saying here? He was saying that He saw within Peter the potential to be a rock, for that is what the name 'Peter' means. Simon was the kind of vacillating character who could walk on the water with Jesus and yet 'followed afar off' when he was on the land. But Jesus had the insight, as do all good counsellors, to see people not just as they are but as they can be.

Lovingly and gently He prods us towards perfection.

This is a characteristic of the Holy Spirit also. He sees us as we are, loves us as we are, but yet loves us too much to let us stay as we are. Lovingly and gently He prods us towards perfection.

How many Simons?

We continue looking at Simon, the Galilean fishermen, the brother of Andrew and the son of John, to emphasise the point we are making, namely, that Christ saw him not as he was but as he could be. And of course everything that Christ did in Simon Peter's life was designed to draw him up to his full height spiritually. This too, as we have started to note, is the way the Holy Spirit works with us. But more of that a little later.

Let's ask ourselves now: How many Simons were there? There were at least three: Simon as his friends saw him, Simon as he saw himself, and Simon as Christ saw him. What was Simon like in his friends' eyes? I can only conjecture, of course, but I imagine his friends might have described him like this: blustering, impulsive, loud mouthed – sometimes even dirty mouthed – but clearly endowed with leadership qualities nevertheless. What was Simon like in his own eyes? Certainly he did not perceive himself as the same man that his friends saw. We never see ourselves as others see us. Indeed, we do not even see ourselves as others see us *physically*. When we look in a mirror the image we see is always reversed. And mentally and spiritually it is the same; it is another self we see from within. The poet Robert Burns said:

> *Oh wad some power the giftie gie us*
> *To see ourselves as others see us!*

To see ourselves as others see us may be helpful, but what is more helpful is to see ourselves as God, Christ and the Holy Spirit see us. They see us, as we have been saying, not merely as we are, with dark marks on our soul, but as we can be – complete in the Godhead.

A minister tells of going to a children's home to give out Christmas presents. Before doing so he spent a little time with the matron in charge, and during the course of conversation asked if the children had someone special who befriended them – an uncle, perhaps, or some other relative. She said that all did, except two. One of the two was a beautiful little black boy whose name was Philip. The matron recounted how one day a chimney sweep came to the home. When little Philip saw his black face he ran to the matron, buried his face in her skirt and cried:

'There's a black man coming.' No sweep was ever as black as Philip, but he had taken his ideas from the other children and, being small, he hadn't seen much of himself. After all, everybody else he saw was white! This story is a parable. We are quick to see in others what we so easily miss in ourselves.

I wonder, was it like that with Simon? Was his picture of himself a flattering one? No doubt he thought of himself as a good judge of other people, a good husband, and perhaps even a good son-in-law. Certainly, he appeared to have a great concern when his mother-in-law was ill (Luke 4:38–44). If someone had said to Simon, 'Are you without fault?' I think he might have answered, 'No, I do have some faults.' But I don't think he would have particularised them. Usually people don't until they are serious in the pursuit of holiness. Then, and only then, will we dig them out, itemise them, pray over them and say, 'This, and this, and this is sin within me.'

> We are quick to see in others what we so easily miss in ourselves.

A reed turns into a rock

We look now at the Simon Jesus saw. I think if we were speaking with full understanding as well as accuracy we would say that our Lord saw *two* Simons. First, Simon as he was (which was neither the Simon his friends saw nor the Simon he himself saw) and, second, the Simon Christ could make of him. The two were so different that they required a different name. Our Lord, looking at Simon, said, 'You are Simon son of John,' and then, envisaging the Simon he could make, said, 'You will be called a rock. That is the man I'll make you' (see John 1:42). What a change: Peter the reed, who could be shaken by even the gentlest wind would, under the counselling ministry of Christ, become a rock.

Did that happen? Most certainly it did. Through the combination of Christ's counselling and later the Holy Spirit's counselling, the impulsive blusterer became clear in judgment and firm in will. Listen to how one commentator describes the changes that took place in him: 'The man who could curse and swear and deny all knowledge of his best friend to save his own skin became a valiant leader at Pentecost and the unshaken champion of the sect which was itself to change the world.'

> He had taken on the characteristics of his Lord.

In 1 Peter 2:1–10, Peter speaks of Christ as the living Stone – rejected by men but chosen by God. It is interesting that Peter talks so much about Christ as being a Rock, for under the tuition of the 'Rock', he himself had become a rock. Not, of course, that Peter could be compared to Christ, but he had taken on the characteristics of his Lord which were foreign to his own nature. 'This is what I will make of you,' Jesus had said, 'a rock.' And He did.

The real you
It is always a powerful moment when one person stands before another and paints for him or her a picture of the kind of person he or she can be. This is something all good counsellors know how to do.

Pardon the personal reference, but when counselling I have often found myself saying something like this to a husband who has told me he felt weak and inadequate: 'In Christ you have the potential to be the man who can strongly move into your wife's world, to be the kind of husband to her that Christ is to the Church – initiating, loving, and considerate.'

I remember on one occasion talking to a woman who had been raped in her teens and was finding it difficult to give herself fully to her husband: 'You believe deep down that because you were violated you cannot now give your attractiveness to anyone. However, in the strength and power of Christ, your femininity which you now want to hide can blossom into an attractiveness that will not only bring out your own inner beauty but *His* also.' The changes those God-inspired remarks made in those people's lives are something I thank God for to this day. To Him be all the glory.

Our Lord's dealings with Simon Peter, particularly in respect of putting before him a vision of what he could be, set a pattern the Holy Spirit follows in His counselling ministry with us. Tell me, have you ever been at prayer and caught a vision, if only for a moment, of what it would mean to be the person you longed to be? That was the ministry of the divine Counsellor at work within you. He sees with double vision, and to get more of that double vision we must determine to spend more time with Him.

Who is the real you? Is it the person you yourself see? No! Positively no! Unless your powers of introspection are heightened by the Holy Spirit, you do not know yourself. Psychology is not enough. Psychologists and psychiatrists can be amazingly ignorant of themselves, and some appear to need the treatment they give to others. Is the real you the person others see? Again I have to say a definite 'No'. It may be an act of faith on my part, but I am ready to assert that the real you is the person the Holy Spirit wants to make you. You were not made to grovel, to be beaten and frustrated by sin. You were made for God Himself, and seated deep in your heart there are longings to know Him and be like Him.

He sees with double vision.

In a zoo some years ago I looked at eagles in their cage. Somehow the sight hurt me. The great birds were made for the skies but here they were, confined in a cage! So many of us are like that – made for higher things but confined in a cage of doubt, fear, denial, perhaps even sin. Just as Jesus looked on Simon the reed and saw Peter the rock, so the Holy Spirit looks on you and sees you maybe as ineffective, beaten, cowed and fearful, but He also sees you as confident, effective, sanctified and strong, moving ahead along the Christian pathway with great strides.

Oh, if only we could see ourselves as He sees us! If only we could move closer to Him, stand at His side and get that double vision – the vision of the men and women we are and the men and women we might be. But what stops us getting close? Mainly it is our unwillingness. When our will is intent on getting closer, we *will* find a way.

The person God meant

The divine Counsellor is at work within us seeking to make us into the kind of person He sees that we can be. Emerson said:

> *Could'st thou in vision see*
> *Thyself the man God meant,*
> *Thou never more could'st be*
> *The man thou art, content.*

How does the Holy Spirit go about the task of enabling us to see the man or woman God *meant*? He can only do it, as we have said, when we get close to Him or allow Him to get close to us. No counsellor is effective unless he or she has the confidence *and* attention of the person being counselled. Sadly, many of us keep the Holy Spirit at a safe distance. Charles Swindoll, when talking to a group of preachers and Bible teachers, said, 'As theologians and teachers of the Word we study the Holy Spirit from a safe doctrinal distance; we are loath to enter into any of the realms of His supernatural workings or even to tolerate the possibility of such. Explaining the Holy Spirit is one thing; experiencing Him another.'

I believe with all my heart that the Holy Spirit yearns to transform us in the same way that Christ yearned to transform Simon Peter (2 Cor. 3:17–18). But the cost is great. It means taking time to develop our relationship with Him. Once we do that, however, He goes to work, inflaming, enlightening, prodding, enticing, and moving us on until the difference in us is so marked that we need a new name. To you now, as to one long ago, the Spirit says, 'You are ... But you shall be ...'

Further Study

1 Sam. 16:7; 1 John 3:1–3; 2 Cor. 3:17–18
1. What does God look on?
2. What does God see us becoming?

1 John 1:7; Rom. 2:4; Psa. 19:12; 90:8
3. What blessings come from walking in the light?
4. What is it that leads us to repentance?

Micah 4:6–7; 1 Cor. 1:26–29; 2 Cor. 5:16–17
5. Can God make something out of nothing?
6. What does it mean to be in Christ?

CHAPTER THREE

NO PRAYER – NO POWER

Luke 5:12–15; 18:1–8
Romans 8:18–27
Ephesians 6:10–20

*'And pray in the Spirit on all occasions with
all kinds of prayers and requests.'*
Ephesians 6:18

We have seen something of the way in which our Lord counselled Simon Peter by painting for him a picture of the man He saw him to be. We noted also that the Holy Spirit, our Counsellor, follows that same pattern in His ministry with us. He too seeks constantly to set before us an image of the man or woman He sees us to be, and the more we give ourselves to Him the more He can give Himself to us.

We look now at another counselling session which our Lord gave His disciples – this time a group counselling session. And we shall consider later how the Holy Spirit, the divine Counsellor, seeks to counsel us in the same way. So look first with me at how our Lord counselled His disciples concerning the subject of prayer. One of many passages in the Gospels in which our Lord

> If we do not pray, we faint.

unfolded to His disciples the power and importance of prayer is Luke 18:1–8. The particular aspect of prayer which our Lord brings out in this parable is that of *perseverance*. We are to pray and not faint.

Often when people are overcome by troubles and trials they find it difficult to pray. Time and time again when counselling I have asked people (never immediately, but at some appropriate moment), 'What's your prayer life like?' More often than not they have responded, 'I find it very hard to pray.' It's not easy to pray when things all around us are falling apart, but hard though it may be to accept, that is the time we ought to pray the most. Indeed, one of the goals of a godly counsellor is to help a person get back to a consistent prayer life, for without one there is little chance of spiritual survival. If we do not pray, we faint.

Escaping from the crowds

Over and over again in the Gospels we catch sight of our Lord counselling His disciples to pray. Why did He spend so much time on this issue? Because prayer opens us to God and to the resources of the Holy Spirit. Like a watch, life has a tendency to run down. It needs rewinding. Prayer rewinds the springs of life by opening our spirits to the Holy Spirit. You don't have to tamper with the hands of a watch to make them go round if the mechanism is fully wound. They go round of their own accord. Likewise, when we are in touch with God through prayer then the Holy Spirit supplies the energy we need to get through every day. And not merely get through, but sail through – victoriously.

Jesus needed to pray. So do we.

Counsellors can never take anyone farther than they have gone themselves, and if a counsellor doesn't know the value of prayer then he or she will not be able to convey that to others. Our Lord is the perfect example of a Counsellor who practised what He preached. In Luke 5:12–15 we read that, following the healing of the leper, the news about Christ's great ministry spread widely until the crowds flocked from far and near to hear His words and be healed of their diseases. But on many occasions, we are told, He escaped from the crowds to pray. Just think of it: Christ ran away from the multitudes to get alone and pray (Luke 6:16). That shows how much of a priority our Lord gave to prayer.

We preachers are far too often crowd-conscious. We run from praying towards the crowds; our Lord ran from the crowds in order to pray. Prayer helps us revise our lives and renew them. Jesus needed to pray. So do we.

Pray! Pray! Pray!

Put quite simply, prayer is the heart of our faith. People have spoken to me over the years and said something like this: 'I am no theologian. Put it to me in the clearest terms: What is the heart of Christian living? How do I grow in grace and power?' Prayer is the way (1 Thess. 5:17). However, I know that many of our ideas concerning prayer are confused, and I know too that many find it difficult to pray, even when no problems are crowding into their lives.

A preacher tells of a woman who told him she was leaving the church and never returning. When he asked why, she said that her daughter had sat for a scholarship, and although she and her little girl had prayed hard, she had not passed. Indeed, not only had she failed to pass but she had come bottom of the list. That proved, the mother claimed, there was nothing in prayer, and because of that she was not attending church any more. The preacher concluded, 'It struck me as I listened to her that I had not taught her much about prayer.' He knew the daughter well and realised she could not have passed a scholarship exam if her life had depended on it. She was a beautiful girl and would go on to fulfil some satisfying role in life, but did not have the ability to gain a scholarship. Think of a mother losing faith in prayer because of that.

Some see prayer as simply the means to get something from God. So they pray only when they want something. You may have heard of the little boy who told his vicar that he didn't pray every day because there were some days when he didn't want anything. What would you think of a friend who turned up only when he wanted something? Is that how we treat God I wonder?

When praying is hard

Even those who see prayer as more than just asking for things often tell me they find it difficult to pray. The need for prayer is apparent, the command to pray is recognised (see Eph. 6:18), but the *longing* to pray is not in them. They have to push themselves to get down on their knees. What a tragedy. The very thing we most need, we desire the least. How can we escape from this impasse?

Thankfully, the divine Counsellor is willing to come to our aid. Paul says: 'The Spirit helps us in our weaknesses' (Rom. 8:26). You will know, I'm sure, that some translations use the word 'Helper' rather than 'Counsellor' in the text which provides our theme – John 14:16 – and I do not object to that for that is precisely what the Holy Spirit does – He *helps*. And never is the Holy Spirit more helpful than when He helps us pray.

At one time I went through a dark period when prayer lost all its appeal for me. I continued preaching and writing in a kind of mechanical way, and as far as I can tell, no one noticed any difference. My words were carefully thought out, my sentences studiously crafted, but they were not soaked in prayer. Then the Spirit drew near and challenged me about my prayer life. 'But I don't *feel* like praying,' I complained. 'Then I will help you,' He seemed to say. He did, and by His grace lit the flame of prayer once again in my heart.

> His grace lit the flame of prayer once again in my heart.

Is the divine Counsellor, I wonder, talking now to you about this very problem? Then ask Him to help you. And do it without any further prevarication – today.

'The Spirit is praying!'

We said that our divine Counsellor helps us overcome any disinclination we may have to pray. Romans 8:26–27 tells us that on some occasions He will actually pray in us and through us. These words spell out one of the most astonishing truths about the Holy Spirit contained anywhere in the Word of God. The Holy Spirit, says the apostle Paul, intercedes for us 'with groans that words cannot express' (v.26).

I find very little has been written about this aspect of the Spirit's work so I can only tell you what I think is meant here. The Holy Spirit (like any good counsellor) does not despise human frailties or reprimand us when we don't know how to pray or what to pray for. Instead, He makes our weakness the reason to plead our interests before God. We all experience occasions when we lack clarity about the subjects for which we should pray, and at such times our prayers are very superficial. Thus the needs we express in prayer are lesser needs, and not the things we really ought to be praying about. But sometimes our divine Counsellor, knowing that prayer brings about God's redemptive purposes, takes up the task of intercession for us 'with groans that words cannot express'. The relationship between God and the Holy Spirit is so close that the prayers of the Spirit need not be audible. The sighs of the Spirit are clearly interpreted by God, because it is for God's own purpose for each one of us that the Spirit is pleading.

On some occasions He will actually pray in us and through us.

It is always an awesome moment when one senses

that one is being prayed *through*. All one can do is to silence every other voice that rises up in the soul and say, 'Hush! The Holy Spirit is praying!'

The groan of God

In John 11:33, we see that our Lord was deeply troubled in spirit. The Authorised Version translates the text in this way: 'Jesus ... groaned in the spirit and was troubled.' God was about to use Jesus to bring Lazarus back to life, yet immediately prior to this momentous event our Lord groaned deep within His soul. Why? Let us consider some words of Dr W.E. Sangster: 'All true progress in this world is by the echo of the groan of God in the heart of His people.' What did he mean? An illustration might help.

In previous centuries, much to our shame, Britain was engaged in the nefarious business of slave-trading. How did it eventually come to an end? Did every Briton wake up one morning and say, 'This is most definitely wrong. We must free the slaves immediately'? No! One man woke up one morning and found the Spirit groaning in his soul. That man was William Wilberforce; he and his friends laboured until that most notable hour in our history when we paid a sum larger than our national debt to free the slaves.

Progress in spiritual things is not mechanical. It does not come from ourselves alone. Progress results from the groan of God in the hearts of His people. Was the groan that Jesus felt as He confronted death God groaning within Him? Was it the spiritual precursor of something mighty and momentous? I think so. If it is true, as Sangster says, that 'all true progress in this world is by the echo of the groan of God in the hearts of His people', then ought we not to ask ourselves: When did we last feel the groan of God in our soul?

Three groans!

We will spend a moment more reflecting on the way in which the Holy Spirit encourages us, as did Jesus, to explore the depths and heights of intercessory prayer. Look again at Romans 8, where the apostle Paul reminds us about three kinds of groans. He tells us there that the whole creation groans (8:22), we ourselves groan (8:23), and the Spirit makes intercession for us with groans that can't be expressed in words (8:26).

First then, *the whole creation groans*. Who can doubt it? Everything that lives is subject to disease: human beings, animals, fish, birds, trees, plants. Life seems strangely poisoned at the fount. Second, *we groan within ourselves*. A.W. Tozer said, 'We have not progressed very far in the Christian life if we have not felt the groan that goes on in creation ... and felt also the groan in our own hearts – the longing to be released from bondage and be with Christ.' This is what 2 Corinthians 5:1–10 talks about – the longing that there is in all redeemed hearts to be free from sin's bondage and corruption: 'For while we are in this tent, we groan and are burdened ...' (v.4). Third, and most astonishing of all, *the Spirit groans within us.* Is the groan of the Spirit the answer to the groan in creation? Is this God's way of ensuring spiritual progress in this world? I think it is.

God's last word is joy, joy, joy!

Three groans! Hear the groan of creation. Hear the groan within yourself. Hear too the Spirit making intercession for you with groans which cannot be uttered. But know this also: God's last word is not a groan. God's last word is joy, joy, joy!

Further Study
1 Chron. 16:11; Luke 11:5–10; 2 Thess. 3:2–5.
1. How does Jesus encourage us to pray?
2. What supports us as we pray?

Isa. 53:10–12; Mark 14:32–36; Heb. 5:7; 2 Cor. 4:10–12
3. What did prayer cost Jesus?
4. How does Paul say we give life to others?

John 16:20–24; Gal. 4:19–20; Psa. 30:4–5, 11–12; Acts 13:52
5. What does Jesus promise?
6. What did Paul long for?

CHAPTER FOUR

FACING REALITY

2 Samuel 11:1–27
John 4:1–26
Galatians 6:1–10
James 1: 12–18

'*But the thing David had done displeased the LORD*'
2 Samuel 11:27

So far we have examined just two aspects of our Lord's counselling approach which we see reflected also in the counselling ministry of the Holy Spirit. First, the way in which He holds out for us the vision of the person God sees us to be, and second, the importance of building a good and meaningful prayer life. Counselling focuses, of course, on many different issues, but the two aspects we have considered are regarded by all those who seek to counsel according to Scripture as pivotal and fundamental.

Another aspect of good counselling, and one which we see demonstrated both by our Lord and the Holy Spirit, is bringing important issues to a head through *loving confrontation*. This involves moving people away from symptoms on the surface to face the significant issues.

Look with me first at how Christ demonstrated this skill in His encounter with the woman at the well (John 4:1–26). How did Jesus get to the root problem in the heart of the Samaritan woman without seeming to invade sanctities? Did He say bluntly: 'Woman, you are living an adulterous life'? No, He pinpointed her problem in a more delicate way: 'Go, call your husband' (v.16). She replied weakly, 'I have no husband.' That was true, He acknowledged, recognising her honesty before touching the ugly areas of her life (vv.17–18). It was just a step from there to confronting her with the real issues for which she needed help, and soon her heart was open and exposed. Christ always saw past the trivial issues to the major ones, and never hesitated, though always respectfully, to bring the hidden things to light.

Handle with care

'In almost every life,' said Dr E. Stanley Jones, 'there is an issue which needs confronting, which becomes the decision point from which we swing toward darkness or toward light – toward spiritual malformation or spiritual transformation. If that central issue is not faced then the process of transformation is blocked. If faced courageously then the process and power of redemption is at our disposal.' Powerful words. If it is true that in almost every life there is 'an issue which needs confronting', then what is to be done about it? It must be faced and faced courageously.

> To confront does not mean to affront.

However, when confronting issues such as sin or moral failure, great care must be taken. We saw how expertly our Lord dealt with the woman at the well. He pointed out her moral need in a delicate way that showed readiness to confront her over her sin but respect for her as a person. Did you notice that Jesus said both at the beginning and end of His probing, 'You are right' (John 4:17–18)? He pointed out the good in her at the very moment He touched the terribly sore depths.

There is a form of Christian counselling known as 'nouthetic counselling', *noutheteo* being the Greek word for to warn, admonish, confront. This type of counselling is strongly confrontational, and some of its practitioners (though not all) appear to be more interested in exposing sin than restoring the sinner. Galatians 6:1 reminds us that where there is moral failure, it is restoration, not exposure, that ought to be the overriding consideration: 'Brothers, if someone is caught in a sin, you who are spiritual should restore him gently.' To confront does not mean to affront.

'The arguments of sin'

One of the abilities of a good counsellor, we have been saying, is to bring important issues to a head through loving confrontation. Note the word *loving*. Some people just love to confront – period. But if confrontation is to be successful, then it must be done in a way that shows a strong detestation of sin but respect for the person. Jesus models the way in which to do this. And so too, of course, does the Holy Spirit.

An old hymn which describes the Holy Spirit as a Counsellor has some lines in it which go like this:

> *Christ is our Advocate on high,*
> *Thou art our Advocate within.*
> *O plead the truth and make reply*
> *To every argument of sin.*

The arguments of sin? What does that mean? Psychologists (with their love of awkward phrases) call it 'the rationalisation of desire'. Let me explain what that involves. One day you find yourself being tempted by something that hitherto you have always resisted. But this time you begin to look at it a little differently. Perhaps you begin to talk to yourself like this: 'The pressures in my life at the moment are so strong that surely a little escape from them can be justified. After all, the world is not a Sunday school. Standards change from age to age. No one can blame me for just one lapse – just one.'

You see how it leads on? That is what the psychologist calls 'the rationalisation of desire', and that is what the hymn writer had in mind when he spoke of the *arguments* of sin.

David's great sin

Keep in mind that what makes temptation powerful is the desire within us for the thing with which we are tempted; '... but each one is tempted when, by his own evil desire, he is dragged away and enticed' (James 1:14). Where there is no innate *desire*, temptation has little appeal. King David knew all about 'the rationalisation of desire', as we can see in 2 Samuel 11:1–27. He wanted the wife of Uriah, one of his officers, and while Uriah was on active service fighting the king's battles, David seduced the woman. Then, fearing the consequences, he 'arranged' the death of her husband and added murder to lust. The 'man after God's own heart' wallowed in sin.

How did he ever get to that point? By 'the rationalisation of desire', by the arguments of sin. It would have happened like this: a sinful thought crossed David's mind. He could not help this, of course, but he dwelt on it when he should have blacked it out. He fed his imagination on it when he should have blasted it with prayer. He told himself later that Uriah had died in the discharge of his duty. Gallant soldiers do fall in battle! And then he married the woman and thought he had resolved the problem. He was a victim of the arguments of sin.

Where there is no innate desire, temptation has little appeal.

David was so self-deceived that on this occasion even the Holy Spirit was unable to get through to him (He will plead but never overpower), and so the Spirit used Nathan as one of His 'temporary assistants'. Nathan's barbed little parable did its work. Soon the wail of Psalm 51 arose: 'Have mercy on me, O God ... wash me, and I shall be whiter than snow' (Psa. 51:1,7).

Further Study

Micah 3:8; Isa. 42:1–4; 2 Tim. 2:24–25; Heb. 4:12–13

1. How should God's servant comfort people?
2. How does Paul tell Timothy to counsel others?

Exod. 32:21–24; 1 Sam. 15:24; Rom. 5:1–5

3. What excuses do I make for my disobedience?
4. How does the Holy Spirit keep us from disappointment?

Psa. 32:1–5; Gal. 6:7–8; Rom. 2:14–15

5. What are the benefits of confessing sin?
6. How does Paul say we can avoid deception?

CHAPTER FIVE.

THE SCRUTINY OF GOD

Psalm 139:1–24
Romans 8:1–11
Ephesians 1:1–14
1 John 1:5–10

'Search me, O God, and know my heart'
Psalm 139:23

A question I have often been asked concerning the Holy Spirit is this: Does the Spirit withdraw from our hearts if we ever fall into sin? I have thought long and hard about this, and I have to say: I don't think so. He is hurt by our sin, even grieved by it, but He remains with us and in us nevertheless (Eph. 1:13–14). Some would *like* to believe that He does leave when we fall into sin, for the thought of a grieved and hurting Spirit residing in the soul greatly increases their spiritual discomfort. Experiencing the sting of one's own conscience when one has sinned is bad enough, but the thought that the Holy Spirit is there in the soul also – hurting, grieved and pained – seems to make the sin more heinous still.

Many years ago, when I was living in the city of Sheffield in the north of England, the local newspaper carried a report about a barrister who had to plead 'invisibility' at the Sheffield Quarter Sessions because he was not wearing a wig and gown. In a British court a barrister (known as an advocate in Scotland) is obliged to wear a wig and a gown in the courtroom otherwise officially he is not present. 'I cannot see you,' said the judge as the barrister arose in court. 'You are invisible to me.'

He is always there.

That, I believe, will never happen in the heart of one of God's children. The Spirit is always 'dressed' for the occasion. He will not desert you. You may grieve Him and turn a deaf ear to Him, and if you do not heed Him it is possible that His voice may grow faint within you. But I don't believe He will leave. We are sealed by the Spirit until the day of redemption. *He is always there.*

The purifying Spirit

The work of the divine Counsellor in pleading against the arguments of sin is perhaps needed more now than at any other time in history. I say this because looseness and moral permissiveness is so commonplace that we Christians are in danger of being brainwashed by the world into lowering our moral standards.

Society tolerates things today that years ago would have brought an expression of absolute horror to most people's faces. Take the area of entertainment. (I speak mainly of the scene here in the British Isles.) On stage and screen where people used to worry about whether or not nudity was gratuitous it is now more or less compulsory. On TV we are treated to the most intimate and shameless sexual disclosures. In sport, brattish tennis players and footballers provide us with displays of loud-mouthed arrogance. Much of sport is marred by vindictive and threatening gestures and talk. Businessmen line up to boast about this or that takeover, and almost everyone in politics seems to be hard at work on self-aggrandising

We Christians are in danger of being brainwashed by the world.

memoirs. Once I watched a TV panel programme during which one person objected to the low standards being accepted everywhere today. A member of the panel retorted, 'But it's only human nature.' That sums up the spirit of the world: 'It's nature and therefore hardly sin.'

This attitude must not be allowed to invade the Church. Many are interested only in the power aspect of the Holy Spirit's ministry. But we must never forget that the Spirit's greatest work is helping us to be cleansed from sin and to overcome sin (Acts 15:9). He is, we must always remember, the *Holy* Spirit.

Sensitivity to sin

Is a sense of sin old-fashioned? Our fathers used to talk a lot about the way the Holy Spirit convicted of sin, but 'conviction of sin' is a phrase we don't use much nowadays. It is true, of course, that earlier generations indulged in the most extravagant descriptions of their own sinful nature, and a glance through old hymn books certainly confirms that. Here is a typical example:

> *Me, the vilest of the race,*
> *Most unholy, most unclean.*
> *Me, the farthest from Thy face,*
> *Full of misery and sin.*

The Christians of a bygone age seemed to *delight* in their depravity. One Victorian commentator tells of a village shopkeeper, a devout member of a local Methodist church, who week by week used the same phrase in his prayers to describe his spiritual condition: 'My soul is a mass of putrefying sores.' Yet he was by all accounts a perfectly honest and upright man. Today we regard such attitudes as 'old-fashioned' and are apt to say with a touch of satisfied complacency, 'We are not at all like that.'

Let us be on our guard, however, lest in our unwillingness to express ourselves in the self-deprecating language of our fathers we grow smug in our attitude to sin. It is perilously possible that without realising it we may have been affected by the tendency of this age to reduce the eternal distinction between right and wrong to a question of taste. 'If we claim to be without sin, we deceive ourselves ...' (1 John 1:8).

Ask yourself now: Am I as sensitive to sin as I think I am?

The scrutiny of God

I want to instil a thought in your mind that I hope will be helpful to you not only now but in the years to come: the safest form of self-examination is that which is carried out in the presence of the Holy Spirit and under the guidance of the Spirit. Some Christians are always examining their hearts and thus become unhealthily introspective. Others never examine their hearts and become spiritually indolent and lethargic.

Spiritual examination ought to be a regular activity.

I know many Christians who examine their hearts every Sunday. They claim this is the best time, when work and other pressures can be dismissed from the mind. Whenever it is performed (and one can hardly get by with less than once a week), first invite the Holy Spirit to be present and to guide. The whole purpose of self-examination is to identify the things that should not be in our lives and to bring them to God so that they may be uprooted. If the Holy Spirit is not invited to the moment of self-examination then it is possible that we could end up in a state of self-pity rather than contrition. The Spirit never moves us to self-pity; the Spirit moves us to repentance. Self-pity is an enemy of repentance because it is an attempt to remove the soul's pain by humanistic means rather than by entrusting oneself to God and His Holy Spirit.

Spiritual examination ought to be a regular activity.

The psalmist had the right idea when he prayed, 'Search me, O God ... See if there is any offensive way in me' (Psa. 139:23–24). Begin with that prayer, wait before Him to see what He will make you conscious of. Then ask God for forgiveness and go out into the day – forgiven and cleansed.

Whose voice?

A central thought has been occupying our minds – the truth that the Holy Spirit, our divine Counsellor, is at work within our hearts pleading against the arguments of sin. He, like our Lord, never hesitates to make us aware of important issues in our hearts, but He does so in the same way that Jesus did – tenderly, delicately and respectfully. Would that all Christian counsellors followed their example.

But tell me now before we move on: Do you know anything about what we have been calling 'the arguments of sin'? Something tells me that you do. Cast your mind back over your life for a moment. Can you recall times when temptation has come to you and you felt some sinful desire rise within you? In the courtroom of your soul did you hear the plea of the arguments of sin? And did you hear another voice also, a voice that was low but clear and insistent, speaking to you of past victories, of the people who love you, of home, of your family, of the Church? Who was that, pleading like a skilful advocate in front of a judge, calling to mind every good point from the past in order to help His case? Do you remember moments like that? Whose voice was it?

Yes, you know, don't you? It was the Holy Spirit – your Counsellor. He was pleading the truth and making reply to every argument of sin. Where would you and I be today, I wonder, were it not for that blessed ministry of the Spirit? What if, when the arguments of sin arose,

He had left us without a word? It doesn't bear thinking about. Jesus loved people enough to plead with them to give up their sin. The Holy Spirit does so too. 'You ... are controlled not by the sinful nature but by the Spirit, if the Spirit of God lives in you' (Rom. 8:9).

Further Study

John 16:7–11; Gal. 5:22–25; 2 Thess. 2:13
1. What happens when the Holy Spirit comes?
2. What is the work of the Holy Spirit?

Luke 5:1–11; Jer. 17:9–12; Rom. 1:18–21; 2 Cor. 13:5–8
3. Where does Jeremiah tell us sinners to go for safety?
4. What is the danger of suppressing the truth?

Jer. 11:20; Psa. 11:4–7; 1 Thess. 2:3–12; 1 Cor. 11:28
5. Who does God examine?
6. How well do I submit to God's scrutiny?

CHAPTER SIX

LIGHT FOR THE PATH

Psalm 25:4–15; 73:23–28
Acts 8:26–40
Romans 8:12–17

'He guides the humble in what is right
and teaches them his way.'
Psalm 25:9

We look now at a fourth characteristic of an effective counsellor – the ability to summarise a confused situation in such a way that the person being counselled sees clearly the direction in which they ought to go. An example of how our Lord demonstrated this ability is seen in the passage before us now.

It was a critical moment in our Lord's career. The loud burst of applause which had been there right from the start of His public ministry was now over. The crowds were melting away, and to many of the disciples, by uttering hard sayings, He had deliberately wrecked His chance of success. Surely He was making things unnecessarily difficult, they must have thought; converts would soon find out for themselves the cost of discipleship. Why frighten them off early with a too-realistic recital of the facts?

No more perplexity, no more confusion.

Discerning the unspoken thoughts of His followers and perceiving the mental and spiritual confusion they were in, Jesus brought the issue to a head by startling them with this blunt remark: 'You do not want to leave too, do you?' (John 6:67). Our Lord's question probably caused the disciples' minds to range far and wide. Who would replace Jesus? Where could one find a satisfactory alternative? Reflectively and with painstaking care Peter considered the possibilities. Would Hillel do? Or

Shammai? Or Gamaliel? No. The Saviour's dramatic question had put the whole issue into clear perspective. Peter's reply was magnificent: 'Lord, to whom shall we go? You have the words of eternal life' (John 6:68). No more perplexity, no more confusion. The Master's piercing question had left them in no doubt about the direction in which they should go.

Light for the way ahead

We have observed the way our Lord pierced the fog in the minds of the disciples by asking a powerful and perceptive question. Time and time again when the disciples seemed unsure about what they should do or which way they should go, Jesus would step in and say something that illuminated the path ahead.

This is the work of the Holy Spirit also. God guides us with His counsel (Psa. 73:24), but it is the specific ministry of the Spirit to apply that guidance to our hearts. 'He,' said Jesus, speaking of the Holy Spirit, 'will guide you into all truth' (John 16:13). It is the Spirit who helps to clarify the issues that puzzle us and assists us in seeing clearly the next step we must take. All of us, I am sure, can remember moments in our life when we dropped to our knees in confusion and cried out, 'Lord, what shall I do now?' And all of us too, I imagine, can remember moments when through the Holy Spirit's

'He will guide you into all truth.'

ministry of guidance that prayer was answered.

Without weakening our personalities and thus making us overly dependent, the divine Counsellor remains at hand to bring clarity and illumination to our minds whenever we need it. That guidance, of course, comes in different ways – through Scripture, through circumstances, through sanctified reasoning or through the Spirit speaking directly to our hearts. But whichever way it comes, the end is always the same – light for the way ahead.

A purpose for every life

Why is it so necessary for Christians to receive divine guidance as we make our way through this world? Because we are carrying out purposes that are not our own. Thus every one of us, if we are to be at our best, must have a sense of instrumentation, of being guided by our God, of fulfilling a will that is ultimate. Francis Schaeffer in a tape-recorded talk I once heard put it like this, 'Christians simply must have a sense of being led.' Without that sense of being led, life hangs at loose ends, lacks a goal and also the dynamic necessary to attain a goal. 'Anybody got a car that is going anywhere?' asked someone at the end of a weekend Christian conference. Everyone laughed, for the question didn't make sense. It sounded as if that person wanted to go somewhere but the destination didn't really matter. Much of our life may be like that – lacking direction and goals. If we lose the sense of being led by the Spirit we become victims of our circumstances. Then we are circumstance-directed instead of Spirit-directed. Guidance by the Holy Spirit is the very essence of Christianity. If there is no sense of leadership we will have no sense of sonship (Rom. 8:14).

In some Christian circles to talk of being guided by the Holy Spirit brings an adverse reaction, as if it were a strange and superstitious thing to be led of God, directly and first-hand. This reaction is most revealing. It shows how content we are to have a knowledge of God but not an acquaintance with God. If we are not being led by God how can we claim to be His sons and daughters? Schaeffer was right; we simply must have a sense of being led.

'If we are not conscious of being guided in our lives day by day,' said Dr C. Jones, a Welsh theologian who lived in the late nineteenth century, 'then we are living at a level that is sub-Christian.' Strong words. But are they true? I think they are. God wants to guide us not only in times of emergency but at all times (Psa. 48:14). One of the blessings of having the Holy Spirit within is, as we have seen, that we gain the sense of being led. And not just the *sense* of being led but the practical benefits that come from it.

How aware are we of this? Something that will surprise us when we get to heaven, I think, is discovering how many times while we were on earth we tried to muddle through on our own instead of entering into and enjoying the direction of the Holy Spirit. I was struck by this statement made to a group of ministers in the United States by an evangelist with a reputation for 'telling it as it is': 'Some of the most active Church leaders,' he said, 'well known for their executive efficiency, people we tend to admire, will have a shock in heaven when in the X-ray light of eternity they will be seen as agitated, half-committed, wistful, self-placating seekers to whom the power and serenity of the Everlasting had never come.'

God being who He is – the Architect of fine detail – He must have a plan, a purpose for every life. If we turn our backs on that idea then, as Dr C. Jones put it, we are at a level that is sub-Christian.

Continuous guidance

After God made each one of us He apparently broke the mould because every one of us is different. Each life has peculiar significance. If we find that plan of God for us and work within it, we cannot fail. Outside of that plan we cannot succeed. To be the instrument of the purposes of God is the highest thing in life.

On one occasion I heard a preacher say that whenever he stands up to preach he reminds himself of a verse God gave him at the beginning of his ministry: 'You did not choose me, but I chose you and appointed you to go and bear fruit' (John 15:16). God gave me that verse also and, like the preacher I heard, I rarely stand up to preach without repeating it to myself. Repeating this verse gives me the sense of being sent, of having the backing of the

Eternal One, and of speaking in a name not my own. But it does something else as well – it lays on me a sense of obligation to surrender and be obedient to the working out of God's plan. It gives life a sense of mission and submission.

To be the instrument of the purposes of God is the highest thing in life.

'Ah, that may be fine if you are a preacher,' I hear you say, 'but what about me? I have not been called to preach.' Maybe not, but you have been called to be an ambassador, an ambassador for Christ: 'We are therefore Christ's ambassadors ...' (2 Cor. 5:20). An ambassador must weigh his words carefully, for they represent the views of his country – he is speaking on behalf of his government. Everyone must feel that sense of being a representative. We are speaking, thinking, acting, in a name that is not our own. That is why guidance is not a matter of the occasional but the continuous.

Mission demands submission

All of us, if we are Christians, must walk through the world with a sense of mission. 'The significance of life,' I have read, 'is determined by the significance of what it is identified with and what it represents.' A sense of mission brings a sense of submission. Instead of making you proud and cocky it has the opposite effect. You feel awed and humbled. You want to walk softly before God.

You are on what has been called 'the adventure of humility'.

The whole thought of guidance, whether it is occasional or continuous, strikes at the citadel of the personality and demands the surrender of self-sufficiency. Mark that, for it is extremely important – guidance demands surrender. That is why some find the subject of guidance intimidating; they don't like the idea of giving up their independence. If we are to be guided, then there must be a shifting from self-will to God's will (Psa. 25:9). That will, not your own, becomes supreme. God's will becomes your constant frame of reference.

Guidance should not be a spiritual luxury for a few souls; it should be the minimum necessity for every Christian. Do you remember the verse: 'Those who are led by the Spirit of God are sons of God' (Rom. 8:14)? Guidance, I say again, is the very essence of Christianity. It gives mission to life. But the mission demands submission.

It's surprising how many Christians there are who, though they know God, know little about His guidance, either occasional or continuous. Hence their impact upon life is feeble. We have seen that God wants to guide us not just sometimes but at all times: '... should not a people enquire of their God?' (Isa. 8:19). But the divine Counsellor's concern for us, I imagine, is the same as Christ's concern for His disciples – to guide and not to override. He wants to guide us yet at the same time create initiative in us.

In the little Welsh village where I was brought up milk was supplied by two farmers who brought it daily to each home on a horse-drawn cart. Villagers would take out their jugs to the milkman and have them filled. I noticed that one farmer would lead his horse from one house to the next. The other had trained his horse to move at a command – stop or go. The first horse was helpless without the step-by-step guide. The other had more freedom.

The Spirit guides us in a way that does not override our personality or weaken it, but brings us to a point of healthy dependency. Some would say that dependency on another is unhealthy. 'You Christians are so weak and lacking in courage,' said a man to me once, 'that you have to look to God before you make any move in life.' He had no idea what he was saying for if he had known how deeply entrenched in all of us is a spirit of independence, he would have realised that one of the biggest struggles we have as Christians is to bring our sinful and stubborn natures into submission to the divine will. Our need to be guided is often, I am afraid, greater than our willingness.

Guidance demands surrender.

Five forms of guidance
The task facing the Holy Spirit of giving us guidance is

similar to that of every thinking and concerned parent. He must guide us, but also develop us as people. To lead us and at the same time produce initiative in us is a task worthy of divine wisdom. 'Many parents are benevolent tyrants,' says a child psychologist whom I know, 'who snuff out all initiative and personality in their children. Guidance must be such that each person is guided into a free, self-conscious, choosing, creative personality.'

These are the general routes to guidance: first, guidance according to the character of Christ. We know who God wants us to be like – He wants us to be like His Son. Anything Christ would not do we should not do. Second, guidance through His Word. He makes the Bible come alive to us, and throws a beam of light on the path ahead. Third, guidance through circumstances – putting us in situations where the circumstances indicate the direction in which we ought to go. Fourth, guidance through the counsel of good and godly people. Fifth, guidance through the direct whispering of the Spirit within us.

This last form of guidance is the one to which we are giving special attention – the direct voice of the Spirit in our hearts. Some look on this method as strange and mysterious. It is capable of being abused, I admit, but it is a form of guidance that is clearly laid down in Scripture. Some call it 'the inner voice'. However, we must always be sure that the inner voice is the Spirit's voice, not our own voice.

'Listen!'

If our divine Counsellor is ready and willing to guide us, how do we recognise His voice when He speaks to us? That is the issue with which we must come to grips. 'My sheep know My voice,' Jesus told His disciples categorically (John 10:3–5). When I go to the telephone and hear my mother's voice, I know immediately who is speaking. I know it is not my sister or my secretary, for I have heard that voice thousands of times during the course of my life. 'Ah,' you say, 'but a voice in your ear is a lot easier to discern than a voice in your soul.' Granted, but there is a way to tune in to the voice of the Spirit and learn to hear His accent in Your soul. Here's how it is done.

Train your spiritual ear to *listen*. When the king complained to Joan of Arc that he never heard the voice of God, she replied, 'You must listen, then you will hear.' 'Then Samuel said, "Speak, for your servant is listening" ' (1 Sam. 3:10). There are two main reasons why people fail to hear the Spirit's voice: their spiritual ears are untrained or they are unwilling. Many of us don't want to listen to the voice of God because we are afraid that if God reveals His will to us, it will be disagreeable. 'Your will be done' becomes 'Your will be borne.'

When you commune with God, give as much time to listening as you do to talking. At first you will not be able to distinguish the voice of the subconscious from the voice of the Spirit, but in time the differentiation will be possible. Sometimes, of course, the Spirit booms so loudly in the soul that His voice is unmistakable. But that is more the exception than the rule. Usually He speaks quietly, and to a soul that sits quietly before Him.

Further Study

Psa. 40:6–8; John 4:31–34; Heb. 10:5–10; 1 Pet. 5:5–6
1. How does the psalmist regard God's will?
2. How does Jesus regard God's will?

Heb. 11:6; John 5:19–20, 30; Rom. 15:1–3
3. How independent was Jesus?
4. How does Paul say we follow the example of Jesus?

Isa. 31:2; Deut. 4:32–40; Heb. 3:7–14
5. What made Israel unique?
6. What must we do 'today' and why?

CHAPTER SEVEN

THE GREAT TEACHER

Matthew 7:15–28
John 3:1–15; 16:5–16
1 John 2:18–27

*'But when he, the Spirit of truth, comes,
he will guide you into all truth.'*
John 16:13

Yet another quality a counsellor should possess is a basic ability to teach. Those who are practitioners of what is called 'non-directive counselling' will, I know, be horrified by that statement as they see counselling not so much as giving people direction, but helping them clarify their own thinking concerning their problems and then come to their own conclusions. There is a lot to be said for this approach as it shows respect for a person's individuality and encourages them to develop their own decision-making processes.

However, true Christian counselling is at times non-directive, and at other times directive. Individuals who are struggling with a problem need clear direction on how to avail themselves of Christ's resources, and to provide that one needs, as I have said, a basic ability to teach. Note the word 'basic'. A counsellor does not need to be an expert teacher, but he or she does need to be able to show a person how to take the steps that lead from where they are to where they should be.

Our Lord, of course, provides the supreme example of what and how to teach. No one can hold a candle to Christ's ministry – either in the Old Testament or in the New. He is seen in the Gospels teaching huge crowds, then at other times small groups. In John 3:1–15 we see Him teaching an individual – Nicodemus – the principles of what we call 'the new birth'. Around 19 such private conferences are recorded in the Gospels, when Jesus is seen closeted with a seeking soul and teaching him or her the steps to effective, abundant living. Our Lord taught as no others have taught – before or since.

Our Lord's authority

Before examining some of the ways in which the divine Counsellor applies to our hearts the teaching of Jesus, we must spend a few more moments looking at why our Lord's great teaching ministry was so powerful while He was here on earth.

The crowds were simply spellbound by the things He said; '... were amazed at his teaching, because he taught as one who had authority ...' (Matt. 7:28–29). A similar verse is found in Mark: 'They were all so amazed ... saying, "Whatever is this?" "It's new teaching with authority behind it!" ' (1:27, Moffatt). Obviously it was the 'authority' with which Jesus spoke that arrested people's attention. Other teachers *quoted* authorities, but Jesus spoke *with* authority. What was that authority? An authority imposed from without? No, it was the authority of the facts. He was lifting up the meaning of life, the meaning of the laws and principles underlying life. He was uncovering Reality – Reality with a capital 'R'.

A good many people make the tragic mistake of regarding Jesus as a moralist imposing a moral code upon humanity which humanity was not made for. But

Spellbound by the things He said.

Jesus was not a moralist in that sense at all. He was the Revealer of the nature of Reality. He revealed first the nature and character of God, and went on to show how the nature and character of God is the ground of God's conduct and ours. He then lifted up the laws of effective living which are written into the universe and into every nerve and tissue of our being, and showed us that there is just no other way to live. It was not imposed idealism but exposed realism. Reality itself was speaking. No wonder it was 'authoritative'. Here was the indicative become the imperative.

The Spirit – our Teacher

Our Lord's expert teaching ministry was not lost to the Church when, after His death and resurrection, He returned to heaven. The Holy Spirit, the divine Counsellor, continues Christ's teaching ministry, and would be here, said Jesus, to bring to the disciples remembrance of all the things the Saviour taught them when He was with them here upon earth (John 14:26; 1 John 2:27).

Most commentators agree that the words in John 14:26 and John 16:13 refer to those who would become involved in the writing of the New Testament – and only those. Whilst conceding that this is the obvious meaning of the text, can it be limited only to the writing of the Gospels and the other books of the New Testament? I wonder can it apply also to those who read and study the Scriptures in every age since the canon of the New Testament was agreed by the Early Church Fathers?

The apostle Paul told us that not only did the Holy Spirit inspire those who wrote the Scriptures but He is present also to help us interpret it. The man without the Spirit does not accept the things that come from the Spirit of God, for they are foolishness to him, and he cannot understand them, because they are spiritually discerned (1 Cor. 2:14). Assuming that to be so, what might be the 'all things' our Lord referred to in the text (John 14:26)?

Before answering that, permit me to draw your attention to the views of a prominent agnostic. The great difference between Christianity and science, he claimed, is that Christianity is fixed but science isn't. Science is open and progressive, he went on to say, because it is not fixed in terms of absolutes and non-optional dogmas.

While this is entirely true, it is not true entirely. In the Person and teaching of Christ we have God's full and complete disclosure. But of course we could not see or comprehend all that is involved in His teaching in one classroom encounter, any more than we could understand mathematics by having a three-hour lesson. The revelation which God has given us through Christ is final in the sense that nothing will be taught that is different from it, but we must see that it is also progressive and unfolding. In what respect? In the way that the Holy Spirit brings out from the words and teaching of Christ new understanding, new challenges and new insights. These are all found in our Lord's words, in embryonic form at least, but the Spirit takes them and leads us to deeper comprehension. The divine Counsellor will teach us all Jesus taught but not other than Jesus taught.

There is another aspect of the word 'all' which I would like to consider with you now, which is this: when we are not under the Holy Spirit's guidance, we can soon become focused on something that Jesus taught and neglect the 'all'. This is a trap any one of us can fall into – and many have. They concentrate on one aspect of Jesus' words and make that the whole issue. Francis Schaeffer pointed out many years ago that the Church in every age has made the mistake of taking some of Jesus' words, putting a fence around them, and claiming a particular emphasis as their own. The consequence of this is a lopsided Christianity with an overemphasis on some things and an under-emphasis on others.

The Holy Spirit brings new understanding

My next statement might be slightly exaggerated but I make it simply for the purpose of illustration: whole denominations are built around one truth. This is not to say they don't believe other aspects of Christian teaching, but the truth they are always emphasising appears to make other truths less important by comparison. They live on *a* truth instead of on *the* Truth. Thus they have to be controversial to justify their lopsidedness. Christians who are truly open to the movement of the Holy Spirit in their lives will be creative rather than controversial.

Being reminded

The Holy Spirit, we must remember, is not only our divine Teacher but also our divine 'Remembrancer'. He promises to bring back to our remembrance all that Jesus said. What does this mean?

It does not mean that the Holy Spirit will magically bring into our minds the words of Jesus if we have not taken the time to read them and ponder them. Some time ago I met a man in Scotland who told me that although he regularly read the Old Testament and the epistles, he never real the Gospels because he believed the Holy Spirit's ministry was to bring home to him the things Jesus said. I pointed out that Jesus promised, '[He] will remind you of everything I have said ...' (John 14:26). *Remind*, I suggested, implies that Jesus' words are already in our memory, and the Holy Spirit's work is to prompt us in ways that make sure we do not forget them. He was unconvinced. He suggested (not in the politest terms, I am sorry to say) that I had lost my

> The Holy Spirit will guide us into all truth.

faith in the supernatural.

The fact that the divine Counsellor is ready to remind us of the words of Jesus (John 15:26) is one of the greatest arguments for soaking our minds in Scripture, particularly the Gospels, where Jesus' words are recorded. The more we expose ourselves to His words, the more easily the Spirit can remind us of them. Just before writing these lines a colleague and I were struggling to come to a decision about an important issue. We didn't know what to decide, then the Spirit reminded us of Jesus' instruction: 'Go the second mile.' We laughed together for we knew that naturally it was not what we wanted to do. The divine Counsellor, however, thought differently.

Truth hurts

The Holy Spirit will guide us into all truth. What does this really mean – guide us into truth? Sometimes a teacher is able to teach a certain truth but is unable to guide someone into it. When this happens in a church setting (a Bible study for example) it is a matter of concern, but when it happens in a counselling session it is even more worrying. A counsellor should be able not only to teach the truth but guide a person into it also.

To be fair, counsellors have a better opportunity to guide individuals into truth than preachers or teachers who present truth from the pulpit because they can ask questions such as these: Do you understand what I have been saying? How do you respond to what I have just said? Counsellors are taught never to present an insight to someone without checking that the person understands what is being said and making sure they are following them every step of the way. Counsellors know too that if they present to someone a truth that is challenging or demanding, the personality more often than not becomes adept at looking for ways of escape. It puts up defences or seeks to minimise the impact of a challenging truth through such means as denial and rationalisation. Thus skill is needed not only to present the truth but to outmanoeuvre the objections, overcome the difficulties, gently rebut the arguments, and thus guide people into possession of the truth.

The Holy Spirit is expert not only in teaching truth but in guiding us into it. I tell you this – you and I wouldn't be where we are now in our spiritual lives unless He had been at work in this way.

The Spirit of truth

Clearly, Christ, when uttering these words was thinking of the truth of His words and the insights He had shared with His disciples, but could the promise mean more than that? Could it be that the Holy Spirit wants to lead us also into the truth about everything that is connected to our lives here on earth?

Think about times in your past when the Holy Spirit has guided you or disclosed something to you that put the truth about a matter into clear perspective. Can't that be understood as the Spirit guiding you into all truth? Have there been occasions in your life when you needed to understand the truth about a matter that was causing you confusion and then, to your surprise, in a relatively short time everything seemed to open up and the fog of confusion was blown away? Who brought that about? Could it have been the Holy Spirit?

I know that kind of situation has occurred a thousand times and more in my own life, but I have never until now thought of it in terms of the Spirit of truth making matters clear.

> Our Lord was an expert Teacher. And so is the Holy Spirit.

Can the promise of being guided into truth be seen also in the way the Spirit opens up a difficult scripture, or the truth regarding both options in a difficult decision? Why can't these be part of the truth which Jesus promised would be disclosed to you and me? Our Lord was an expert Teacher. And so is the Holy Spirit.

Further Study

Matt. 24:35; John 5:24–27; 2 Cor. 1:18–22
1. Whose words can we always rely on?
2. What does Paul say we can be sure of?

Luke 24:27, 44; Eph. 3:2–5; 1 Thess. 1:4–6
3. What is the theme of the Old Testament?
4. How did Paul receive revelation?

Prov. 2:3–11; Acts 15:22, 25, 28; Phil. 1:9–11
5. How did the apostles reach agreement?
6. What does Paul pray for?

CHAPTER EIGHT

'BEING THERE'

Matthew 17:1–11
Isaiah 66:5–13
Acts 2:29–39
2 Corinthians 7:1–16

'As a mother comforts her child, so will I comfort you …'
Isaiah 66:13

The last (but not least) qualification of a counsellor that we shall consider is this – the ability to come alongside someone who is hurt and support them in their pain – 'being there for someone'. One illustration of our Lord 'being there' for His disciples is seen in Matthew 17:1–11. It is suggested by the simple but intriguing phrase 'after six days' (v.1).

There is, of course, a distinct connection between this verse and the events immediately preceding (Matt. 16:21–28). Dr G. Campbell Morgan deduced that when the disciples discovered their Master was going to a cross, they drew back in dismay. Follow the clue in the words 'after six days' carefully, he advised, and it will be seen that during this period there was a sense of estrangement between the disciples and the Master. Peter, at one point, had gone so far as attempting to dissuade Christ from even thinking about going to a cross. Christ's foretelling of His death seemed to make the idea of Messiahship impossible. The disciples wanted to reign with Jesus; He wanted to go to a cross.

The six days of confusion would be ended by the act of Transfiguration, but what must it have been like for our Lord and His disciples as they walked together through the northern part of Israel? He, no doubt, was pained by their failure to understand, and they were pained by the revelation that their concept of Messiahship did not appear to match His. But did He leave these dull and misunderstanding disciples and go it alone? No, He stayed with them. He was there for them even when they were not there for Him.

Being there is not giving advice; it is saying in non-verbal ways, 'This is not the time for talking but, as far as I am able, I want to bear the pain with you.'

I remember being faced with a distressing problem early in my Christian life. Everyone I consulted suggested there must be some sin in my life, otherwise I would be free from problems. I felt towards them as Job

He was there for them even when they were not there for Him

must have done when he said, 'I have heard many things like these; miserable comforters are you all!' (Job 16:2). Finally, a man who was an incurable stutterer and unable to complete a single sentence started to put his arm around me, and then drawing back placed his hands

together in an expression of prayer as if to say, 'I can't help you on the verbal level, but I will be there for you in prayer.' That meant more to me than any words. It was non-verbal, but empowering all the same.

I once talked to a man in South Africa who told me that his wife had made his life almost impossible for a number of years. She humiliated him in front of friends, telephoned his boss and told lies about him, ran up debts that he was expected to pay, and ill-treated him in a whole host of other ways. 'How are you handling all this?' I enquired. His reply moved me deeply, 'My only wish is that I might be able through a Christlike attitude to give her a taste of how much God loves her, and, above all else, my longing is to be there for her until she leaves this world for eternity.' I thought as I listened, 'Why, you could almost put those same words on the lips of the Holy Spirit.'

Counsellor and *Comforter*

Let's face it, some of the problems we encounter are not going to go away no matter how hard we pray. So what sort of help can we expect to receive from our divine Counsellor? He will be there for us – empowering us with His comforting presence, sharing our pain and entering into all our sorrows.

The translators of the New International Version, the version I have used in this book (though in my personal study I much prefer the New King James Version) were all scholars. When deciding upon a name in English for the Holy Spirit they therefore leaned towards a word that suggests the giving of advice or verbal direction. This is not said in any derogatory way or to suggest that the translators were not men of feeling. But I have often noticed when going through the NIV that the translators chose words with an intellectual ring – words which seem to be lacking in feeling. For instance, 2 Corinthians 5:14 is translated 'Christ's love compels us' in the NIV, whereas the NKJV translates it, 'The love of Christ constrains us.' See what I mean? The word 'constrains' has a feel (in my opinion) which the word 'compel' does not have.

The Greek term for the Holy Spirit is *parakletos*, derived from *para* (beside) and *kaleo* (call), and means 'one who comes alongside to help'. I wish the word could be translated 'Counsellor and Comforter' – a phrase which would convey the fuller idea that the Holy Spirit is not just someone who gives us advice but someone who feels *for* us and *with* us also. Oh, He *feels*, does this blessed Counsellor and Comforter. And more than we will ever know.

The ultimate Counsellor

The Holy Spirit is a Counsellor who does more than give us advice; He enters into our hurts, empathises with our pain, and is there for us in every difficult situation of life. Listen to how the Amplified Version translates John 14:26: 'But the Comforter (Counsellor, Helper, Intercessor, Advocate, Strengthener, and Standby), the Holy Spirit, Whom the Father will send in My name ... He will teach you all things.'

The Holy Spirit is a Counsellor who has everything. The ability to give good advice? Yes. The ability to empower with divine strength? Yes. The ability to be our Advocate? Yes. The ability to pray through us when we don't know what to ask in prayer for ourselves? Yes. The ability to stand by us when we are overcome with worry? To comfort us? Yes! Yes! Yes! There isn't a single thing we need in life that He isn't able to provide.

The word Comforter – *con* (with) and *fortis* (strength) – means one who strengthens you by being with you. It's astonishing what strength we draw from someone just being with us when we are going through a painful experience. Prior to her death my wife spent many hours sleeping. At first I would steal away to my study and work after she had gone to sleep, but she told me on one occasion that even in her sleep she could sense whether or not I was there. 'Just being there,' she said, 'just sensing you are at my side is more of a comfort to me than I can ever explain.' I have had the same thought at times in relation to the Holy Spirit, haven't you? Simply sensing He is at our side is a comfort that we can never explain.

The Spirit's first work

There are those who claim that the *first* task of the Holy Spirit is not really a work at all. Primarily, they say, He is there to be with us. What He does in us and through us is important, but His primary service is *to be there for us*.

If this is so (and it is difficult to argue against it), then we must see that our preoccupation with gifts rather than the Giver is entirely out of place. Many Christians seem to be more taken up with possessing the gifts of the Spirit than possessing the Holy Spirit Himself. He is the gift, and although we are instructed by Paul in 1 Corinthians 14:1 to 'eagerly desire spiritual gifts', this does not mean that we are to think more highly of the gifts than the Giver. Peter talks about the Holy Spirit being *the* gift (Acts 2:38). He is the gift of gifts, and when He is with us and in us then He supplies us with the gifts that enhance our spiritual effectiveness.

Early in my Christian experience I made the mistake many make today. I was brought up in a church where a great emphasis was placed on the gifts of the Spirit but little on the Giver. Thus I went over all the gifts mentioned in the New Testament – the gifts in Romans 12, those listed in 1 Corinthians 12, and those mentioned in Ephesians 4. I then laid out my shopping list before the Lord and said, 'Father, these are the gifts I want from You.' The Spirit whispered to my heart, 'Are the gifts more important than the Giver?' This gentle rebuke helped me to see that I was more interested in the gifts of the Spirit than the Spirit who gave the gifts. This is a danger we must all avoid.

'Trust my love'

There are occasions in life when problems don't go away despite our most ardent praying. At such times the divine Counsellor ministers to us His comfort and supernatural strength.

Just before writing this I recalled a vivid memory of when I was a little boy being taken to hospital to have my tonsils removed. When I entered the place, smelt the distinctive smell that hospitals had in those days, saw the white-coated nurses and doctors, I became very frightened. Looking up into my mother's face I said, 'Do I have to go through with this? Will it hurt? What is it all for? Will I die under the anaesthetic?' Well, what can you say to a small boy about to have such an operation? My mother could have given me all the medical reasons why the operation should be performed, but I would not have understood. So she simply said, 'I can't save you from it, my dear. For your own good this has to be done, but some day you will understand. You must trust my love. I shan't leave you and I will be here waiting for you when you come out of the anaesthetic.'

I will be with you all the way.

That boyhood experience has been a parable to me. There have been many times in my life (and I am sure in yours also) when the Holy Spirit has whispered in my soul, 'I cannot shield you from this. You will have to go through it, and you may feel some pain. But I will be with you all the way.' Job never got the answers he wanted to his questions, but he received something better: he came through his experiences with a richer sense of God's presence than he had ever felt before (Job 42:1–17).

Further Study

Isa. 63:7–9; Eph. 3:14–19

1. What are the kindnesses of the Lord?
2. What does the Holy Spirit do in us?

Isa. 43:1–7; Luke 12:11–12; 2 Tim. 4:16–18

3. When does Jesus say the Holy Spirit will help us?
4. What strengthened Paul?

Deut. 8:10–18; 1 Thess. 5:16–22; Acts 4:31; Gal. 5:18–21

5. What must God's people never forget?
6. How does Paul admonish his readers?

CHAPTER NINE

SUPERNATURAL COMFORT

Psalm 86:1–17
Isaiah 49:8–16
Acts 9:19–31

*'Shout for joy, O heavens … For the LORD
comforts his people and will have compassion
on his afflicted ones.'*
Isaiah 49:13

The comforting ministry of the Holy Spirit is not simply a theory; it is a glorious fact. Who, reading these lines, has not felt the divine Counsellor's consoling presence steal into their souls during a time of personal difficulty or distress?

Early in my ministry I thought it was my task alone to bring comfort to people who were disheartened. However, I remember on one occasion receiving a gentle rebuke from the Lord that put the matter into its true perspective. As a young minister, every week seemed to bring its batch of special difficulties and duties. I confess there were times when my spirit rebelled. Constant contact with people who were plunged into sudden tragedy and horrendous pain drained me of nervous energy. This drove me, of course, to prayer, but sometimes my prayers became complaints. I said to the Lord, rather petulantly I am afraid, 'I can't keep going into the homes of tormented people who are repeatedly submerged in sorrow, give them sympathy and talk about a God of love.'

We comfort; He is the Comforter.

It was then that God spoke to me and reminded me that above and beyond any comfort I could give was that of the Holy Spirit. His work was to bestow not human comfort but *supernatural* comfort. I must do my part and trust Him to do His. When I realised that Another was ministering along with me to the sick, the suffering, and the bereaved, I began to relax and turn over the major part of the task to Him. All who belong to Christ's Body are expected to minister comfort to each other, but the biggest share belongs to the Holy Spirit. We comfort; He is the Comforter.

Grace – simply amazing

How reassuring it is to know that when we need comfort and consolation the Holy Spirit is more than equal to the task. Others can *bring* us comfort but He *is* comfort. A classic example of how the Spirit ministers grace and comfort in the midst of difficulty is found in 2 Corinthians 12:1–10.

Paul doesn't tell us what his problem was but uses a metaphor – a thorn in the flesh – which is used elsewhere in Scripture to convey a troublesome issue.

A special supply of His comforting grace.

Many have speculated about that 'thorn' but no one knows for sure what it was. Opthalmia? Epilepsy? Neurasthenia? A harassing evil spirit that stirred up strife everywhere he went? We don't really know. One preacher joked that Paul had a thorn in the flesh and no one knows what it was; if we have a thorn in the flesh everyone knows what it is! Paul asked the Lord three times to take it away but the answer was 'No'. The problem was to remain. But in the midst of his trouble God began to pour into Paul a special supply of His comforting grace; grace to accept the 'No', grace to endure the discomfort and grace to handle the pain.

But how does grace work? Like this: you find yourself undergoing a period of testing and your heart becomes heavy. You lose your appetite, struggle with insomnia, and become increasingly irritated. Then you go to prayer. As you pray the heaviness in your spirit continues, but then suddenly, it is as if a weight is lifted from you. You breathe more easily and your spirit feels a little lighter. What has happened? Some might call it 'a spontaneous sense of relief'. Those who know call it grace.

In a fallen universe like this we are confronted with issues which produce almost inconsolable pain. Sir Arthur Conan Doyle tells in his autobiography what made him a materialist in early life. As a physician he constantly saw sights which he could not reconcile with the idea of a merciful providence. He tells of going into a humble home where there was a small cot, and by a gesture made by the mother he sensed that the problem lay there. He picked up a candle, walked to the cot and stooped over it, expecting to find a young child. What he saw, he says, was a pair of brown sullen eyes full of loathing and pain which looked up in resentment to his. He could not tell how old the creature was. Long thin limbs were twisted, the face malignant. 'What is it?' he asked in dismay. 'It's a girl,' sobbed the mother. 'She's nineteen. Oh, if only God would take her.'

What answer can we give to explain circumstances such as that? There is no adequate answer. It's easy to brush perplexing matters aside and say they are the result of living in a fallen world, but that still leaves huge issues unresolved. Why did God allow sin to strike the universe in such a way? Could He not have modified its consequences so it would not have affected us as it has? These are easy questions to ask, but even if God gave us clear answers I am not sure we would be able to understand them. We will understand everything one day, but meanwhile God simply says, 'Here's My comfort, you can get by with this.' In moments of bewilderment it is not answers we need; it is comfort. That comfort may not keep us blithe but it will keep us brave. 'For the LORD comforts his people and will have compassion on his afflicted ones' (Isa. 49:13).

When the world goes grey

Sooner or later every one of us needs comfort. It does not matter how strong we may be, how composed and free from sentimentality, the time will come when we need to feel God's solace. The Holy Spirit is the minister of grace. He is the One who brings into our hearts the resources of the Godhead. Let us never forget that.

Some, when needing comfort, turn to drink. But there is no real comfort to be found in the cup. Too much champagne at night produces real pain in the morning. Drink can no more cure our sorrows than an anaesthetic can cure a cancer. Robert Burns, Edgar Allan Poe and others have tried it and discovered that it only aggravates the trouble it was taken to heal. Others turn to literature. 'The anodyne you need,' they say, 'is reading. Relief can be found in a library. Turn for consolation to the infinite resources of literature.' I love literature and have made it a habit to read several books a week. But in the time of real sorrow there is no adequate comfort in books. Some comfort perhaps, but not enough to heal a heart that is torn. Is Dickens your favourite author? You will not find him very comforting when the doctor diagnoses a serious medical problem. Do you like Scott? The Waverley novels will not be very effective on the day you come home from the cemetery.

> The only sure comfort when all the world has gone grey is the comfort of God.

What about nature, or music, or art? They can be helpful supplements but they can never be substitutes. They are not a fount of comfort in themselves. I can tell you from a lifetime of facing trials, including bereavement, that the only sure comfort when all the world has gone grey is the comfort of God. '... you, O LORD, have helped me and comforted me' (Psa. 86:17).

Is optimism enough?

There are in the Christian Church those who advocate optimism as the way to approach life's problems. You sometimes see posters outside churches designed to catch people's attention with a cheerful word. But those who choose the words for some of these posters, as well as those who display them, seem to have no understanding of what is relevant to the needs of the general public. Once I was on my way to a home that had been stunned by an awful bereavement, wondering what I would say to the distressed family. As I passed a church I caught sight of a large poster that advised: 'Cheer up – it may never happen.' I remember shouting out in my car: *But it has happened.*

There is no lift in optimism in an hour like that. Like the nerveless needle of a broken barometer it continues to point, even in a thunderstorm, to 'Very Fair'. No, the only reality we can depend upon in the hard and cruel world is the consolation of the Holy Spirit.

One of the things that saddens me about the day in which we live is that few people read the biographies of the early missionaries any more. Many of them contain dramatic instances of the way in which the Holy Spirit comforts and consoles. Take Allan Francis Gardiner for example, the intrepid missionary to South America. He and his companions found themselves on Picton Island in the most difficult circumstances imaginable. It is hard to read the story without tears coming to one's eyes. Yet in his diary he wrote, 'Great and marvellous are the loving kindnesses of my gracious God to me.' Many things may be absent. But God's comfort. Never.

Wait till you get home

We have been emphasising that we are not always going to receive answers to the difficult questions that arise during our lifetime. Questions such as these: Why has God allowed this? What possible good can come from it? How can a loving God permit such a thing? A good deal of frustration can be avoided if we settle for the fact that God knows what He is doing and that one day, not now but when we get to heaven, all will be made clear and 'He will wipe every tear from their eyes' (Rev. 21:4).

I heard a minister tell how when he was a boy he went to a youth camp for a month. Within a few days he had run out of money. The incident occurred earlier in the century when few people had telephones, so he sent a telegram to his father saying: 'S.O.S. More money please.' To his surprise no answer came. The first week ended and still there was no answer. The second began and slipped away, again without an answer. His friends noticed his preoccupation and began to explain his father's silence in their own way. 'He has forgotten you are here,' said one. 'He is too busy to bother with you,' decided another. A third claimed, 'He is trying to teach you a lesson.' Then one of his companions asked him, 'What do you think yourself?' He thought for a moment and said, 'I don't really know. But I'm willing to give him the benefit of the doubt. I think I'll wait until I get home and ask him myself.' When he did return home the whole matter was explained in one or two sentences. His father told him, 'You needed to learn the value of money. Hard though it was for me, I saw this as the best way I could teach it to you.'

The answers you don't get here, you will get in eternity. Here, however, you are guaranteed the strength you need to carry on.

What happens now?

We end our meditations on this note: as we make our way towards heaven life may be hard and perplexing, but God has given us His Holy Spirit to be our Counsellor along the way. And what a Counsellor He is! Run your mind back with me over the characteristics of this matchless Counsellor which we have looked at.

(1) He seeks to draw out of us all the potential which God has built into us, and is continually at work developing us into the kind of persons God sees us to be.

(2) He prods us to prayer, and on those occasions when we don't know how to pray as we ought He takes over and prays in us and through us.

(3) He brings hidden things to light in our souls and seeks to rid us of all sin.

(4) He shines the laser beam of knowledge and wisdom through the fog that sometimes

surrounds us, and guides us in ways of which we are both conscious and unconscious along the path He wants us to take.

(5) He teaches us as no other could teach us, and leads us into the thing our hearts were built for – truth.

(6) He comforts us whenever we are in need of solace, and strengthens our hearts to go on even though we have no clear answers to our predicament.

How sad that with all the resources of our divine Counsellor available to us we prefer so often to muddle through on our own. When we refuse to open up to Him, to depend on Him and consult Him, we deprive ourselves of the love, wisdom, and spiritual sustenance we need to live effectively and dynamically. He will open up to you, but only if you will open up to Him (James 4:8). Believe me, take one step towards Him and He will take two towards you.

Further Study

Matt. 26:36–46; Phil. 4:4–7; Psa. 27:1–6

1. What did Jesus pray three times?
2. How does Paul suggest we cope with anxiety?

2 Cor. 4:7–18; Heb. 12:1–3; 2 Pet. 3:13–18

3. On what do we fix our eyes?
4. What are we waiting for?

Isa. 61:1–3; Heb. 2:16–18; Psa. 37:39–40

5. What is the good news?

6. What does our High Priest do for us?

NATIONAL DISTRIBUTORS

UK: (and countries not listed below)
CWR, Waverley Abbey House, Waverley Lane, Farnham, Surrey GU9 8EP.
Tel: (01252) 784700 Outside UK (44) 1252 784700

AUSTRALIA: CMC Australasia, PO Box 519, Belmont, Victoria 3216.
Tel: (03) 5241 3288

CANADA: Cook Communications Ministries, PO Box 98, 55 Woodslee
Avenue, Paris, Ontario.
Tel: 1800 263 2664

GHANA: Challenge Enterprises of Ghana, PO Box 5723, Accra.
Tel: (021) 222437/223249 Fax: (021) 226227

HONG KONG: Cross Communications Ltd, 1/F, 562A Nathan Road,
Kowloon.
Tel: 2780 1188 Fax: 2770 6229

INDIA: Crystal Communications, 10-3-18/4/1, East Marredpally,
Secunderabad – 500 026.
Tel/Fax: (040) 7732801

KENYA: Keswick Books and Gifts Ltd, PO Box 10242, Nairobi.
Tel: (02) 331692/226047 Fax: (02) 728557

MALAYSIA: Salvation Book Centre (M) Sdn Bhd, 23 Jalan SS 2/64,
47300 Petaling Jaya, Selangor.
Tel: (03) 78766411/78766797 Fax: (03) 78757066/78756360

NEW ZEALAND: CMC Australasia, PO Box 36015, Lower Hutt.
Tel: 0800 449 408 Fax: 0800 449 049

NIGERIA: FBFM, Helen Baugh House, 96 St Finbarr's College Road,
Akoka, Lagos.
Tel: (01) 7747429/4700218/825775/827264

PHILIPPINES: OMF Literature Inc, 776 Boni Avenue, Mandaluyong City.
Tel: (02) 531 2183 Fax: (02) 531 1960

REPUBLIC OF IRELAND: Scripture Union, 40 Talbot Street, Dublin 1.
Tel: (01) 8363764

SINGAPORE: Armour Publishing Pte Ltd, Block 203A Henderson Road, 11–06 Henderson Industrial Park, Singapore 159546.
Tel: 6 276 9976 Fax: 6 276 7564

SOUTH AFRICA: Struik Christian Books, 80 MacKenzie Street, PO Box 1144, Cape Town 8000.
Tel: (021) 462 4360 Fax: (021) 461 3612

SRI LANKA: Christombu Books, 27 Hospital Street, Colombo 1.
Tel: (01) 433142/328909

TANZANIA: CLC Christian Book Centre, PO Box 1384, Mkwepu Street, Dar es Salaam.
Tel/Fax (022) 2119439

USA: Cook Communications Ministries, PO Box 98, 55 Woodslee Avenue, Paris, Ontario, Canada.
Tel: 1800 263 2664

ZIMBABWE: Word of Life Books, Shop 4, Memorial Building, 35 S Machel Avenue, Harare.
Tel: (04) 781305 Fax: (04) 774739

For email addresses, visit the CWR website: www.cwr.org.uk

CWR is a registered charity – number 294387

Trusted
All Over the World

Daily Devotionals

Books and Videos

Day and Residential Courses

Counselling Training

Biblical Study Courses

Regional Seminars

Ministry to Women

CWR have been providing training and resources for Christians since the 1960s. From our headquarters at Waverley Abbey House we have been serving God's people with a vision to help apply God's Word to everyday life and relationships. The daily devotional *Every Day with Jesus* is read by over three-quarters of a million people in more than 150 countries, and our unique courses in biblical studies and pastoral care are respected all over the world.

Prayer – A Fresh Vision

Prayer is our pathway to intimacy with the Father –
without it we simply cannot grow. If we want to
know God and draw closer to Him, then we need to
be in conversation with Him.

Selwyn Hughes looks at the basic building blocks
of effective prayer, using the greatest example of all –
Jesus Christ.

£6.99 (plus p&p)
ISBN: 1-85345-308-0

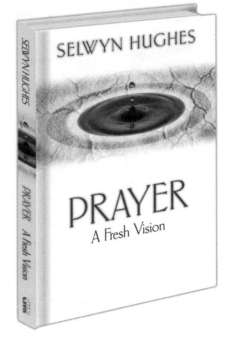

The Scandal of Grace

Grace has been described as a scandalous doctrine, an undeserved privilege given to us by a loving God. It's amazing and it seems too good to be true! In this book discover how to accept the grace of God for every situation. Learn how to pass God's grace on to others and enter the freedom that it brings.

£6.99 (plus p&p)
ISBN: 1-85345-299-8

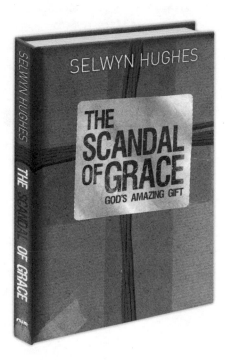

Heaven Bound

Is heaven a 'solid' place to you that feels like home? Or is it vague, ethereal and not quite real?

We can be 'so heavenly minded we're no earthly good', but Christians who did the most for this world thought a great deal about the next one. What evidence is there that heaven exists, and how can we taste its reality now? What is heaven like, and what goes on there?

In *Heaven Bound* Selwyn Hughes masterfully answers these vital questions and brings the insight of over 50 years of teaching to a subject rarely addressed:

- Cope with the tension of being a 'pilgrim-ambassador'

- Be anchored and secure in a turbulent world

- Find the faith and love that spring from heaven's hope

£6.99 (plus p&p)

ISBN: 1-85345-267-X